Lipstick Love Sonnets

John McAteer

Copyright ©2022, John McAteer

ALL RIGHTS RESERVED.

No part of this publication may be reproduced, stored in a retrieval system, or transmitted in any form or by any means—electronic, mechanical, photo-copy, recording, or any other—except for brief quotation in reviews, without the prior permission of the author or publisher.

ISBN: 978-1-955622-59-2

Published by
Fideli Publishing, Inc.
119 W. Morgan St.
Martinsville, IN 46151

www.FideliPublishing.com

Contents

Sin 1

The Mist 3

Dreams 5

Shadows 7

The Mind 9

My Dog 11

The Scar 13

Hunger 15

Whisper 17

Seat of Silence 19

Secrets 21

Smile 23

Rain 25

Darkness 27

Peace 29

Vision 31

Forgotten Words 33

Regrets 35

Hopeful 37

Life 39

The Road 41

Solitude 43

Lies 45

Honor 47

Loss 49

Path 51

Comfort 53

Clouds 55

The Decision 57

Magic 59

Soul 61

Purpose 63

Open Door 65

The Bend 67

Measure 69

The Rose 71

The Sigh 73

Solace 75

Holding 77

To My Family

Sin

The passion of lust is only heightened by sin,
    and I have tasted it on many elusive nights.

The clouded mind only wants what it cannot have, a stolen
    moment of heated bliss is worth the loneliness of never
    being able to caress it.

Time doesn't give back to you what you have not earned,
    so take your passion as the road unfolds your path, and
    never looked back.

The Mist

The fog was rolling in, and I could taste the salt in the air as I watched the waves crash on the sandy beach.

I thought of you and your lustful touch as the emptiness filled my thoughts, it was easy to look back but impossible to go forward.

I remember the first time we kissed as we exchange the breath of life.

I know now that you had to leave me and I miss you every day.

I hope the sun is shining on you.

My lips will always remain dry until we meet again.

Dreams

Pieces of a dream were developing in my mind and transferring me to a very special time.

The bottle was empty, but my heart was full, and there you stood just as a shadow in my door.

I was quaking, as I was afraid of waking only to find an empty dream like a fragrance that overcomes your senses and tries to hold on to you forever.

But forever is always just around the corner from reality.

Hold on to the precious gems that life puts in your path.

Love your empty dreams and hope they will visit you on dark and lonely nights before they take flight to start a new day.

Shadows

When the days are the darkest and the nights they seem to last a year, you can always count on me to be near, like a shadow that never leaves you.

I have looked back, only to find confusion.

Comfort was always what I was looking for — a kind word, soft touch, a gentle caress.

My shadow is a portrait of my life, both good and bad.

I embrace the solitude and remember that failure is only a stepping stone to success in love and life.

The Mind

The beauty of your mind is it never ages.

It is your vehicle from the day you enter this earth and the curse of old age.

Your mind can be seen as a time machine transferring you back to a place of joy or trauma.

It can be like an aphrodisiac to your aging body, making your dreams and wishes that they are, and transporting you to where you can embrace the joy of love.

Your mind is your never-ending story and a road well-traveled, so pack light and make every day a journey.

My Dog

The inspirational journey of love and heartbreak is found in all shapes and sizes, as was the true love that I had for my dog.

She loved me, understood me, comforted me and, yes, she even took me for a walk, never judging me just unconditional love.

Like everything in life, there is a beginning and an end for all of us, but my dog has given me far more than I could have imagined.

She has gone to a better place now, and although my heart aches, I thank God for what she gave me — love, respect, and my greatest memories.

Those are what I cherish the most.

Till we meet again, my eternal love.

The Scar

The scar of loss is a mirror image that we must all face and cherish — this is a testimony to what we have been through.

Emptiness is a shadow that must be filled with treasured memories.

The tears of joy are the same as pain, only the scar will always remain.

Hunger

The passion of love is a feast for your mind,
   and a deadly desire that will follow you forever.

The hunger for the dark and what it brings is just part of the
   secrets that we keep locked deep inside.

A door that will never be opened is a door with only one
   side.

Each day will bring you a new hunger, this is how it is served
   is up to you.

Whisper

The treasured sound of a whisper is a magical moment between two people, it flirts with all your senses and pulls you into a place that will dance in your mind forever.

The words of a whisper are not as important as that heated breath of air as it seeps into your ear.

Your mind only hears what it wants to hear — desire.

Seat of Silence

When I meet the man of my dreams, we will cherish each single moment, love life and each other, just a small reflection of inner peace.

Nights spent in each other's arms as we lay in the somber silence of the dark, just staring at each other.

We did this for 30 years, as you embraced my inner soul.

Our favorite restaurant was one thing we always cherished — same table, same seat.

Today I went back to our favorite restaurant and sat at the same table, only to share my table with a seat of silence.

You will always be in my heart and in my mind.

Until I see you again, I will save you a seat by the window.

Secrets

The secrets of life and love are so complex — both equally hidden in the shadows.

The secrets that we hide and lock inside are nourished, sometimes by the shadows of darkness and lies.

In some cases though, your secrets can become the foundation of your personality and are engraved into your future setting you on a path that you will never change, never share.

Secrets, they are the forbidden fruit that only you can own.

Smile

The softness of the smile has the strength of forever and gives you inner peace that hides many loving emotions.

The hidden facial beauty that a smile brings, the joy to a lost soul as you cherish the joy of the moment.

Remember to smile and put to rest the frown, they are two separate characters that cannot share the same stage.

Rain

The serenity of dancing rain on my roof has painted many a beautiful vision in my mind.

I draw my eyes closed to a somber night of sleep, a prelude to the storm.

The rain is the earth's purity, as it washes away the sins of nature and refreshes the soul of the earth.

Remember the salt of a tear is like the rain, they will grace you with a hidden emotion.

Darkness

The hunger of silence is always served alone, and shared with the shadow of darkness.

Someone once said, "Tell me your deepest secrets and I will lie and tell you mine."

Inner peace is very rarely found, because the fear that haunts us, letting us expose our deepest thoughts.

Peace

The open box on the floor was calling me to surrender my soul.

It was the last memory I had cherished with you.

I was always afraid to look at it.

Tormented by the loss of you, I stayed away from the room with the open box on the floor.

With any open box, the secret of its contents is no longer a mystery.

Vision

To see clearly you must have a vision that will challenge you to push harder in life.

Your eyes will ingest many beautiful things, and some truly horrible images.

Your vision will become your barometer for how you go forward because it will transform you to an image of the past and allow you to prejudge the future due to either a good or a bad flash back.

Seeing is believing and believing is seeing, so embrace it.

Forgotten Words

The breath of life is only exchanged with a passionate kiss.

The rush of your lips as they say, "I love you" will be branded in your mind.

I will always be there as you hold your love in your arms.

The fulfillment of your deepest desire, as you gaze into each other's eyes.

Love is the shadow you cast as you forget the forgotten promises of years gone by.

Never let go of your dreams or the forgotten words, or your love will be lost on the road to loneliness.

Regrets

I swallowed the guilt of loneliness as I gave in to the darkness, hoping to find a path back to you.

As I search the sharpened edges of a scarred heart.

The drama has concluded, and the curtain has closed.

I have had many regrets, but loving you was not one of them.

As I await my final quest, I leave you with only a shadow of memories of the past and the promise that we will meet again.

Hopeful

Being an optimist gives you a corrected path and a personality pondering whether the glass is half full or half empty.

Step out of your comfort zone and dabble with the unknown desires, and maybe shed your inhibitions and fear.

Maybe, or should I say hopefully, find a path to happiness rather than sharing a boring story that will only fall on a deaf ear.

Life

The sun will rise and set to many backdrops in your life, some sweet and some casting deep scars that can never be healed.

The struggle to find your way is only carved out by your will to persevere.

Some can be balanced.

But, the true weight of life is trying to balance your visions.

Some will crumble.

Who will you be the strong-willed wolf or the sheep going to slaughter?

Leave your fear at the front door and enter the house, there you will find only love.

The Road

Your life is a never-ending journey where each step will take you father into your dreams.

Thru it all, you will follow the road map that has been preordained from your birth with no stops along the way.

The scenery will change, friends will come and go, but you will still travel in only one direction —forward.

So, strap yourself in and hope your travels are blessed.

Solitude

The solitude of silence is a great blessing.

What is yesterday without today?

We all feel the wind and the sun, but can you feel what tomorrow brings as we face a new day?

As they say, prepare for the worst and hope for the best.

Always look for a better path and never fall prey to the shadow of your fears.

Lies

Sit down beside me and let me tell you some lies, because the only way to love me is to look deep in my eyes.

Lies have no shadows and can never be remembered once they have passed your lips.

So, look inside of yourself and chase only what you want to hear.

Will it be truth or just another hidden path to endless dark nights?

So, sleep well and remember:
only the truth will calm your soul.

Honor

To cherish a dream, you must honor the concept of failure but never give in to the loss.

Your drive is your ability to persevere once you have challenged your soul.

You will honor your commitment to yourself and the people around you.

No greater blessing can you bestow than to honor what God has given you.

Loss

There are many twists and turns in what we call life, but none as bad as emptiness and loneliness.

This is the hollow hole that devours your ability to find peace.

It gives you your ability to travel into the basement of life where most people stay because they are unwilling to travel back up into the light.

Never fear what gives you pain because scars heal and this will bring you forward into a better day and a brighter light.

Path

Once someone touches you inside and caresses your heart, no one can replace the true feeling of love.

Once you have lost your true love, it seems like the sun never wants to shine.

Trying to fill the void is very hard and promises to be a long path, but in life your destiny will be uncovered.

What you have lost will become just a heartbeat away from comfort.

Comfort

A love of lies is a hollow hole of darkness that can never be kindled by the warmth of the sun and the joy of true love.

Caress and hold onto the one who can comfort your mind and your heart.

Let the flow of life fill your emptiness and draw you into a special place.

Clouds

Symbolism is always surrounded by unknown questions, like clouds as they form before a storm.

Like the cascade of rain that can purify the air we breathe or a cold chill on a cold winters day.

We treat life and love the same way, one is a challenge the other a mystery that we can chase or look for all our lives.

Clouds may form, but never lose sight and follow your heart until you find your warmth on that cloudy day.

The Decision

Life is beautiful as it draws some very hard truths to the surface of reality.

The love and joy that once filled your heart becomes twisted with a cruel compromise, like watching a clock that never moves or a moment that turns into a horrible memory.

It is the decision to let go, only to crave what you will always truly miss.

Honor the decision that you make in life, even if you don't agree with your choices or your loss.

Magic

I once pondered how a magician could make an item disappear and then make it return as if it was never gone.

Some losses are never gone, as your mind fills the void of loss.

This is the only thing that keeps you attached to the past and its precious memories.

Love lost is love remembered.

Never forget the hidden beauty that once filled your heart with joy.

Soul

Have you ever had the darkness of the night talk to you as you lay in bed and ponder your life?

I have tried to process both the precious moments and the dark ones as they each share a purpose.

Not everything in life can be happy.

The tears of grief are shed to cleanse and build the hope of a better tomorrow.

Your journey in life is simple, live each day as it unfolds, face life with the knowledge that there is always someone there to hold your soul.

Purpose

Never close your eyes to the darkness, as you will be blinded twice — once by never seeing the shadows of love, and second by shutting out any chance of finding your future.

Your destiny is a course that you must face with no expression, just conviction.

Use the treasures of tomorrow and crumpled pieces of heartache with happiness, it's how you will survive.

Put the jaded pieces together and try to reshape your life.

Open Door

My journey was long, and at times lost in a cloud of confusion.

Finding your path is a like walking through a revolving door — it changes with each revolution.

Your heart is like an open door to love and pain.

You will never know what can unfold unless you pass the threshold of the open door.

Will you find sunlight or darkness?

Every journey has to have a beginning.

Always remember: love hard, never hurt the one who has penetrated your heart and rested in your soul with the warmth and the strength of yesterday.

Lead them into your tomorrow with the promise of tenderness and love.

The Bend

My iron horse was running and the desert was calling me.

The air was dry, and I was hungry for the open road.

A new life was calling me and I embraced the possibility of new love and memories.

My old life was now just a shadow in my rearview mirror, just a reflection of pain and loss.

Now, I will follow the sun and not give in to the darkened corners of the unknown like the bend in the road that hasn't come yet.

Measure

A grain of sand is no more than an empty time capsule in your life, it will always be there for the next generation to analyze.

Your life is a grain of sand in the scheme of life and love.

Most of us are put on this earth to find our path, but the illusion is how to find our destiny.

For me, my path was to love my soulmate and get her through the hardest time of our life, which was just a different grain of sand and another mystery to solve.

The Rose

The thorn on the rose is a reminder to proceed with caution.

The heart is like a rose, beautiful but yet it needs understanding.

Once you have been pierced by the thorn, it leaves you with a second site just like your heart.

They say the heart can only be healed again once it finds true love, like the prick from a thorn that you will remember.

The Sigh

The sigh of passion is quiet, yet it says so much.

Hidden deep inside, but it only exposes itself when the breath of life is exchanged through a long, unforgiving, passionate kiss that is always looking to follow a never-ending journey, one that you are always looking to chase as it can devour you.

When you chase the unknown, it can be more than a challenge.

Solace

The solace of the night is like a never-ending puzzle we strive to solve.

Viewing all the dark shadows that life gives us, only to realize that they will follow us into the next dark moment that comes at a price but is not always found.

So, travel light, and find comfort in knowing that your greatest achievement is when the moment becomes a memory.

Holding

The endless caress is like a shadow that can never pass through your door.

Only your hidden desires can gain access to what was once a dream of passion.

That dream holds your mind hostage for eternity, only for it to follow you into the darkness.

The still of the night confesses to your feelings, so your mind can feed your rocking chair as your path unfolds to the years of aging.

www.ingramcontent.com/pod-product-compliance
Lightning Source LLC
Chambersburg PA
CBHW061745290426
43673CB00095B/271